Show The Giant Within

Simple Hacks to be Real-Life Hero

Show The Giant Within

Simple Hacks to be Real-Life Hero

HEMANG C. PAJWANI

Worldwide Published by
Pendown Press

PENDOWN PRESS
An ISO 9001 & ISO 14001 Certified Co.,
Regd. Office: 2525/193, 1st Floor, Onkar Nagar-A,
Tri Nagar, Delhi-110035
Ph.: 09350849407, 09312235086
E-mail: info@pendownpress.com
Branch Office: 1A/2A, 20, Hari Sadan, Ansari Road,
Daryaganj, New Delhi-110002
Ph.: 011-45794768
Website: PendownPress.com

First Edition: 2021
Price: ₹259/-
ISBN: 978-93-90557-84-4

Disclaimer: This book is designed to provide information on "facts about blood/platelets and organ donation." It is sold with the understanding that the author is not engaged in rendering any professional services. Every effort has been made to make this book as complete and accurate as possible. However, there may be mistakes, both topographical and in content. Therefore, this text should be used only as a general guide and not as the ultimate source of facts about blood/platelets and organ donation. Furthermore, this book contains information on facts about blood/platelets and organ donation that is currently only up to the printing date. The purpose of this book is to educate and entertain. The author shall have neither liability nor responsibility to any person or entity with respect to any loss or damage caused, or alleged to have been caused, directly or indirectly, by the information contained in this book.

Layout and Cover Designed by Pendown Graphics Team
Printed and Bound in India by Thomson Press India Ltd.

CONTENTS

I dedicate this book to all those youngsters who wish, but hesitate to give blood/platelets/organ donation. They are the ones who always motivate me to donate.

THE BEGINNING

Hemang Pajwani

Hello My Name is Hemang Pajwani, an Instrumentation Engineer by education,. entrepreneur by Profession and by passion "A volunteer Platelet donor", a Motivational Speaker for "donating Blood and platelets."

In 1993, I completed my Graduation in Instrumentation Engineering and joined a job with a handsome salary. Suddenly, my father had a massive heart-attack in 1995, but by the grace of God he survived, but could not resume our family business of "Pharmaceutical Distribution in Mumbai" on a regular basis. Ultimately I left the job of my engineering field and joined shoulder to shoulder with my elder brother for Family business. And now I am a successful businessman in the Pharmaceutical Industry.

During Engineering, I studied in Hostel and one fine night, when I was sleeping in my room with my roommates, one unknown person knocked on our room's door and asked me to join him at the hospital. I was shocked and asked "Who are you? Why should I join you? " But, after watching my Hostel Dean with him I was relaxed. Later, he explained to me the complete scenario and I understood the value of Blood donation for the first time ever in my life. One 7 years' old baby girl was suffering with Thalassemia and she was in urgent need of blood from an "O negative blood group donor."I remembered that at the time of college admission I had mentioned my blood group in the form. After donating Blood I was feeling proud of myself for helping someone, whom I was not knowing and might never meet ever. At that time I came to know one of the secrets of becoming "A real-life hero."

And from that day, my journey as a Volunteer Blood Donor, started and I committed myself to give blood donations regularly. But due to the "O negative Blood group" I can not donate without an emergency. Up to April 2013 I have donated blood maximum 5 times only.

In April 2013 I met Mr. Mehul Doshi through our common friend Mr. Bakulesh Thakkar. He guided me and suggested that I should start a Platelet Donation in Tata Memorial Hospital, Mumbai, the most leading and reputed hospital for Cancer treatment In India. It was the first time I came to know about the platelet donation and my journey of Platelet Donation started since 15/04/2013. Till the date of the publication of this book (31/01/2021) I have donated Platelets 168 times and the journey will continue till I can able to maintain good health (does not get diagnosed as diabetic, or some other diseases that make me unfit to donate blood) or law of India permits.

Blood is needed to treat the accident victims, cancer patients, trauma induced surgeries, orthopedic/cardiovascular surgeries, pregnancy complications and in many more medical emergencies also. Platelets are used for cancer, trauma, burn and surgery patients to assist with blood clotting and stop internal and external bleeding. It is useful in treating Dengue patients also. Even in some incidences operations/surgeries get delayed due to non-availability of Blood/platelets.

In the current scenario awareness of Blood/Platelets donation and its need are not much explored. Ultimately it's always a shortage of Blood/Platelets to treat patients. One of the biggest challenges is the shelf-life of blood and Platelets are 42 days and 5 days respectively. Means, once Blood/Platelets get donated it should be consumed before it gets expired.

Its simple solution is to spread awareness of platelet donation and youngsters should come forward to donate as and when required. As of now we have almost 700 volunteer donors in Tata Memorial Hospital who regularly donate platelets and as of now 85% of the total need of Tata Hospital is fulfilled by volunteer donors only. (as per July 2020 Records)

I am giving you Bold promise that "if all the healthy citizens of India come forward to donate blood/platelets there will be zero death, no delay in operations due to lack of blood/platelets.

We can be the First country in the world who might be able to fulfill complete blood/platelets needs of the country. In the whole world India can be known/recognized as "Country of the Millions of real-life heroes."

And now I am on a mission to make India "the country of the Millions of Real-life heroes" by 2025 where there will be zero incident when any operations/surgeries will be delayed due to unawareness of Healthcare Education and non-availability of Blood/platelets.

INTRODUCTION

HOW CAN YOU BE A REAL LIFE HERO?

Contrary to the popular belief, you need not be a spiderman or shaktiman, nor you need to wear a cap, or even be a politician. Simply put, if your acts are heroic, you will emerge as a hero for sure.

1. **Let go of the ego of yours:** The first and foremost thing that you should do is to let off your ego. You should not attach certain price with yourself. Make yourself available for the right cause and right people, without attaching a Self Tag.
2. **Initiate the particular shift you wish to determine:** Thought without action is like abortion. If you are determined for something, say plantation drive in your area, some economic activities that will provide mass employment, some move for the environment, etc., do not move about the right moment or something called "favourable condition."
3. **Take responsibility of your failure give credit to someone else for the success:** Initiate something big that will create a big impact on the people around you. Pursue your

plan consistently, learn how to take optimum use of the people around you, try to achieve the desired outcome in a specified amount of time. If the plan turns out to be a fiasco, come forward, take the responsibility(of your failure). But, when your plan becomes successful, take credit to someone else in your group.

4. **Be prepared to act when others are actually passive:** Do not act like average. Be the front runner. When you believe in something, stick to it. Do not let your determination die down, simply because most of the people are opposing it. If you can clearly see you goal, rest assured, you will achieve it. Mind, at the initial phases, you will find most of the people talking exactly the opposite. But, as you refuse to budge, and keep on doing the things, uninterruptedly, you will achieve both—the target as well as the confidence of the people.
5. **Perform arbitrary actions associated with kindness:** The act of kindness is independent of an auspicious moment. If you see politicians' kindness related actions at the time of election, or a famous person in your area distributing clothes on his or her birthday, do not get the impression (wrong) that kindness' actions are occasion-bound. Just start doing acts of kindness. Arrange tuition fees for a poor student, buy a noon-time meal for your needy rather than offering income, take an aged neighbor to a healthcare appointment, donate blood/platelets.
6. **Do not Advertise your Accomplishments:** You may find it paradoxical, but it is irrefutably true. You need not do anything for your society with a motive. You should not think like "As I want to be a hero, I must give charity, actions related to kindness and advertise every feet of accomplishment." Instead, think like "I am committed

to the welfare of my people. I will keep on doing good things, irrespective of what people think about me. For me, kindness is not an investment. It is true." If you evolve your mind and become altruist by nature, rest assure, you will emerge as a hero.

- **Donate Blood/Platelets:** Educate people about how their blood/platelets can help save lives. Set example of your own. Donate blood. Educate near and dear one about the fundamentals of healthcare and stand beside them whenever they are in need.

ACKNOWLEDGEMENTS

I am grateful to my wife Alpa, My daughter Khushee, Mr. Bakulesh Thakkar, Mehul Doshi. Last but not least, I wish to thank my friends—Hitesh, Hemal and Manisha, who always motivated me and stood beside me during my platelets donation journey and the book- making. I owe them a great deal of gratitude.

Special thanks are due to those who gave their time to read/ edit my manuscript, including Dr. S.B. Rajadhyaksha (H.O.D.), Dr. Anisha Navkudkar (Consultant), and all team members of Department of Transfusion Medicine, Tata Memorial Hospital, Parel, Mumbai. Your honesty, suggestions and advice helped me refine ideas and approach throughout the creative process. This book is richer with your contributions.

I am eternally grateful to Akshar Yadav, Dinesh Verma and his entire Pendown Press team for printing my book.

KNOWLEDGE BYTE 1

BLOOD DONATION

"It takes 15 minutes to be
A Real-Life Hero–Donate Blood"

World Blood Donor Day is celebrated every year on June 14 to thank blood donors who save lives every day. It also encourages people all over the world in order to donate blood voluntarily.

October 1 is recognized and celebrated as the National Voluntary Blood Donation Day in India to raise awareness about the importance of blood donation.

Why do I emphasize so much on blood donation?

Every year our nation requires about 5 Crore units of blood, out of which only a meager 2.5 Crore units of blood are available.

The gift of blood is the gift of life. There is no substitute for human blood.

Every two seconds someone needs blood.

Every two seconds someone needs blood.

More than 38,000 blood donations are needed every day.

A total of 30 million blood components are transfused each year.

The average red blood cell transfusion is approximately 3 pints.

The blood type most often requested by hospitals is Type O.

Sickle cell and Thalassemia patients can require frequent blood transfusions throughout their lives.

More than 1 million new people are diagnosed with cancer each year. Many of them will need blood, sometimes daily, during their chemotherapy treatment.

A single car accident victim can require as many as 100 units of blood.

Examples of Blood requirements

Incidents	Tentative units required
Automobile Accident	50 units of blood
Heart Surgery	6 units of blood / 6 units of platelets
Organ Transplant	40 units of blood / 30 units of platelets
20 bags of cryoprecipitate	25 units of fresh frozen plasma
Bone Marrow Transplant	120 units of platelets/ 20 units of blood
Burn Victims	20 units of platelets

Why Donate Blood?

A blood donation truly is a "gift of life" that a healthy individual can give to others in their community who are sick or injured. In one hour's time, a person can donate one unit of blood that can be separated into four individual components that could help save multiple lives.

From one unit of blood, red blood cells can be extracted for use in trauma or even surgical patients. Plasma, the liquid part of blood, is administered to patients with clotting problems. The third component of blood, platelets, clot the particular blood when cuts or other open wounds occur, and are often used in cancer and transplant patients. Cryoprecipitate anti-hemophilic factor (AHF) is also used for clotting factors.

The blood which you donate will be utilised by accident victims, people suffering from critical blood disorders like sickle cell, haemophilia, and even cancer patients. All the donated blood units are tested for diseases like HIV, hepatitis, syphilis and other infections to make sure that these diseases do not get transmitted from one person to another.

Donating blood is a noble act which saves many lives. On an average, an individual can donate blood every 3 to 4 months. However, this limitation varies for different blood components, as in case of platelets one can donate them after every 3 days but not more than twice a month and only 24 times in one year. Make a habit of donating blood regularly and encourage others to do the same. In our country, where there is a critical shortage of donated blood, each donation matters.

How much blood does a normal human body have?

There are around 10.5 pints (5 liters) of blood in the average human adult body, although this will vary depending on various factors. During pregnancy, a woman may have up to 50% more blood.

The average quantities of blood are:

About 9 pints (4.3 liters) of blood in an average-sized female

(5 feet 5 inches tall and weighing 165 pounds)

About 12.2 pints (5.7 l) in an average-sized male (6 feet in height and weighing 200 pounds)

In an infant, about 1.2 fluid ounces (fl oz) for every pound of body weight (75 – 80 milliliters (ml) of blood per kilogram).

In a child, about 1–1.2 fl oz for every pound of body weight (70–75 ml of blood per kg)

How much blood can you lose or donate?

The standard amount of blood a person will give during a blood donation is only one unit (about 350 ml./450 ml.). This is around 10% of the blood in the body and a safe amount of blood to donate. The reason there is a limitation on how much blood a person can donate in one go is because there is a limited amount of blood in each one's body which depends upon various factors such as weight, age and height of the person. When a person donates 1 unit, that much amount and its components can be recovered by the body, within a span of few hours to weeks without affecting the health of the donor.

Who can donate blood?

There are several parameters that determine the eligibility of an individual to donate blood. Guidelines laid down by the Ministry of Health, Government of India have to be followed by blood banks and organizations conducting blood donation camps.

- **Overall health:** The donor must be fit and healthy, and should not be suffering from transmittable diseases.
- **Age and weight:** The donor must be 18–65 years old and should weigh a minimum of 45 kg.
- **Pulse rate:** Between 50 and 100 without irregularities.

- **Hemoglobin level:** A minimum of 12.5 g/dL.
- **Blood pressure:** Diastolic: 60-90 mm Hg, Systolic: 100-140 mm Hg.
- **Body temperature:** Should be normal, with an oral temperature not exceeding 37.5 °C.
- The time period between successive blood donations should be a minimum 3 months (males) and 4 months (females).

Individuals under certain conditions are deemed ineligible to donate blood:

- A person who has been tested HIV positive.
- Individuals suffering from ailments like cardiac arrest, cancer, epilepsy, kidney etc
- A person who has undergone ear/body piercing or tattoo in the past 1 year.
- Individuals who have undergone immunization in the past 1 month.
- Individuals treated for rabies or received any vaccine in the past 1 year.
- A person who has consumed alcohol in the past 24 hours.
- Women who are pregnant or breastfeeding.
- Individuals who have undergone major dental procedures or general surgeries in the past 6 months.
- Women who have had miscarriage in the past 6 months.
- Individuals who have had fits, tuberculosis, severe allergic disorders in the past.

- Individuals who currently have asthma with active symptoms, and severe asthma patients.

Is it safe to donate Blood?

Yes, it is completely safe. All tubing, bags and the needle used to collect your blood are new, sterile and used only once for you. After use, the entire disposable kit is discarded.

How to prepare for Blood donation?

Just like platelets donation, blood donors will need to get a good night's sleep on the night leading up to their donation. Unlike donating whole blood, you are required to avoid aspirin for 48 hours before donation (only after consultation with your physician), as it will affect the clotting properties of your blood. Doctors also recommend that donors should drink fluids and have a full meal prior to your donation.

Stretching the stomach with a full meal opens the blood vessels around the stomach and constricts them in the rest of the body, resulting in an increased blood pressure. This helps you better tolerate a donation.

How does the blood donation process work?

Donating blood is a simple thing to do, but can make a big difference in the lives of others. The donation process from the time you arrive until the time you leave takes about an hour. The donation itself is only about 8-10 minutes on average. The steps in the process are:

1. **Registration**

   You will need to complete donor registration, which includes information such as your name, address, phone number, and donor identification number (if you have one).

You will be asked to show a donor card, driver's license or two other forms of ID.

2. **Health History and Mini Physical**

   You will answer some questions during a private and confidential interview about your health history and the places you have traveled.

   You will have your temperature, hemoglobin, blood pressure and pulse checked.

3. **Donation**

   Doctor / Technician will cleanse an area on your arm and insert a brand–new, sterile needle for the blood draw. This feels like a quick pinch and is over in seconds.

   You will have some time to relax while the bag is filling. (For a whole blood donation, it is about 8-10 minutes. If you are donating platelets, red cells or plasma by apheresis the collection can take up to 2 hours.)

   When approximately a pint of blood has been collected, the donation is complete and a staff person will place a bandage on your arm.

4. **Refreshments**

   You will spend a few minutes enjoying refreshments to allow your body time to adjust to the slight decrease in fluid volume.

   After 10-15 minutes you can then leave the donation site and continue with your normal daily activities.

   Enjoy the feeling of accomplishment knowing that you have helped to save lives.

What should I do after donating blood?

- Drink an extra four glasses (eight ounces each) of non-alcoholic liquids.
- Keep your bandage on and dry for the next five hours, and do not do heavy exercising or lifting.
- If the needle site starts to bleed, raise your arm straight up and press on the site with a sterile gauze piece until the bleeding stops.
- You might experience dizziness or loss of strength, use caution if you plan to do anything that could put you or others at risk of harm. For any hazardous occupation or hobby, follow applicable safety recommendations regarding your return to these activities following a blood donation.
- Eat healthy meals and consider adding iron-rich foods to your regular diet, or discuss taking an iron supplement with your health care provider, to replace the iron lost with blood donation.
- If you get a bruise: Apply ice to the area intermittently for 10-15 minutes during the first 24 hours. Thereafter, apply warm, moist heat to the area intermittently for 10-15 minutes. A rainbow of colors may occur for about 10 days.
- If you get dizzy or lightheaded: Stop what you are doing, lie down, and raise your feet until the feeling passes and you feel well enough to safely resume activities.
- And remember to enjoy the feeling of knowing you have helped save lives!
- Schedule your next appointment.

How long will it take to replenish the pint of blood donation?

The plasma from your donation is replaced within about 24 hours. Red cells need about few weeks for complete replacement. That's why at least 12-16 weeks are required between whole blood donations.

Blood Shelf-life?

Your gift of blood may help up to three people. Donated red blood cells do not last forever. They have a shelf-life of up to 42 days.

Myths and Facts about blood donations

Myth: Health deteriorates after donating blood.

Fact: If you are healthy prior to donation, your recovery is complete in a day or two. It is advised to rest a while after donating. Drinking enough liquids replaces the lost fluid within a couple of hours. The body produces new cells faster after a donation.

Myth: Taking medication means that one cannot be a blood donor.

Fact: Depending on the medication being taken, it may make you ineligible to donate (temporarily or permanently), though in many cases it won't prevent a donation. Person in charge or the nursing staff should be informed before donating.

Myth: Giving blood hurts.

Fact: The pain experienced is no more than a needle prick. The slight soreness that maybe where the needle was is just a reminder of the good deed done.

Myth: Age is a deterrent to blood donation.

Fact: The age criteria for blood donation is 18-60 years and upto 65 years for regular donors

Myth: You cannot take part in sports or other physical activities after donating blood.

Fact: Giving blood does not interfere with ability to perform physically. Advice to avoid heavy lifting or strenuous workouts for the rest of the day is given after the donation. You can get back on track the next day.

Myth: Giving blood is time consuming.

Fact: The time taken for a single donation session is normally not more than an hour.

Myth: Being a vegetarian, means that the blood does not have enough iron and cannot be donated.

Fact: Vegetarians can donate blood. The iron needed is taken from body stores and once a balanced diet is maintained is replaced after donation. This usually normally takes a month or so.

Myth: HIV or other infections can be contracted from donating blood.

Fact: A clear procedure exists for taking blood from each donor. Sterility is maintained at all steps. A sterile, new needle is used for each donation and is then properly discarded. Use of sterile equipment and technique limits the chance of infection.

Myth: There is limited blood in the body and it is unhealthy to give some away.

Fact: Only about 350-450ml of blood is taken during a donation session. There is enough blood in the body to donate it without any ill effects. The body makes new blood after donation.

Myth: Heavy people are healthier and have more blood give.

Fact: Being overweight makes people less healthy. Overweight people do not have more blood.

Myth: When there is a requirement, blood can be manufactured.

Fact: Blood is not something that can be manufactured. It can only come from healthy human beings.

Myth: Being of mixed race precludes blood from being helpful.

Fact: Race and caste have no bearing on eligibility being a blood donor. It is the blood group that is of importance.

Myth: Blood donation can tell if one is HIV positive.

Fact: HIV antibodies can take months to develop after infection with the virus. Those recently infected may have a negative test result and yet be able to infect others. It is better not to donate blood if at risk of getting HIV or other infections.

Myth: If you smoke, you cannot be a blood donor

Fact: You can donate even if you are a smoker. However, you must be at least 18 years old and weigh at least 45 kilograms. Also, you should avoid smoking for three hours after donating blood and also stay away from alcohol for 24 hours prior to donating blood.

Myth: Donating blood makes the immune system weak

Fact: There is no such lasting danger to the immune system when you donate blood. While the Red Blood Cells return to normal within a few days, the White Blood Cells take a few weeks. However, if the body finds itself in danger, they can be produced quickly.

Myth: Blood donors become obese

Fact: Blood donation doesn't affect your body weight at all, it remains unchanged unless you decide to reward yourself with too much junk post-donation–and that, my friend, is your responsibility and has nothing to do with blood donation, so stop finding excuses.

Myth: People who weigh heavier are eligible for donating blood, those who weigh lighter aren't

Fact: What even? As long as you weigh above 45 kgs, donating blood has nothing more to do with your weight–only because a person below that weight would probably have to face relatively more weakness issues than a person who is above 45 kgs. Also, your weight has nothing to do with the amount of blood your body produces!

Myth: If you're diabetic, blood donation isn't for you

Fact: You cannot donate blood only and only if you take injections to fix your diabetes, like insulin. You CAN donate blood if you control your diabetes with the help of lifestyle changes and oral medicines. Those who have heart problems from type 2 diabetes, however, might not be able to donate in exceptional cases.

Myth: High BP patients cannot be blood donors

Fact: Those with blood pressure between 140 mm Hg systolic and 90 mm Hg diastolic can very well donate blood. This frame might be considered high, but it does not isolate you from donating blood. Moreover, blood pressure medicines do not interfere with the process at all.

Myth: People with seasonal allergies don't qualify for donating blood

Fact: Seasonal allergies do not interfere with blood donation, just like any other mild cold and cough does not affect your daily routine. So, "I have a cold," is an absolutely lame excuse for not giving your blood to someone who needs it.

Myth: Blood donation isn't for women

Fact: Well, whatever is ever FOR women? No, seriously, how does blood have anything to do with gender? Women bleed every month anyway, so they shouldn't? The logical argument could be that women have a lower haemoglobin count than men due to their biological setup. Women naturally survive in lower haemoglobin levels. So, blood donation affects them the same way that it would affect a man. Thus, unless women are pregnant, lactating, anaemic, or suffering from some medical issue that lowers haemoglobin count–they can donate blood.

Myth: A blood donor is prone to infections

Fact: A fresh needle is used for each blood donor. So, there is no chance of an infection that is usually assumed to be transferred from needles–like HIV–from blood donation.

Myth: One day of rest is needed after donating blood

Fact: You can resume your daily activities almost right after donating blood as long as you make sure you drink enough water and juices to replenish your body fluids. You should also avoid alcohol and direct sunlight for 24 hours. But, donating blood doesn't give you enough of an excuse to bunk your daily chores!

"You don't need to have a medical degree
to save lots of a life. Just a good degree of
humanity. Give Blood. Save Life."

KNOWLEDGE BYTE 2

PLATELET DONATION

"Be a Real-Life Hero. Give Platelets to Guard and save someone's life"

What is platelet donation and how platelets are used?

Platelet donations are a special type of blood donation. Our blood is made up of different parts, also called components: red cells, white blood cells, plasma, and platelets. Of the four, platelets are considered a precious resource.

Platelets are tiny, colorless, disc-shaped particles circulating in the blood, and they are essential for normal blood clotting. Platelets are critically important to the survival of many patients with clotting problems (aplastic anemia, leukemia) or cancer, and patients who will undergo organ transplants or major surgeries like heart bypass grafts. Platelets can only be stored for five days after being collected. Maintaining an adequate supply of this lifesaving, perishable product is an ongoing challenge.

Why do patients need platelets?

Platelets are very fragile, short lived blood cells that are essential for normal blood clotting. They must be transfused within 5 days of donation which makes it necessary for us to provide hospitals with a fresh supply of platelets daily.

Platelets are often used to treat:

Cancer patients

Accident victims

Patients with blood disorders

Bone marrow transplant patients

Dengue patients

What are different types of Platelet Products?

There are Random donor platelets (RDP) & Single donor platelets (SDP). RDP is obtained by processing whole blood donation. One unit of RDP contains $>5.5X10^{10}$ platelets with a volume of 50-70ml. An adult patient would require 6 to 8 such units at a time to correct thrombocytopenia. A SDP is obtained from a single donor by aphaeresis technology. Volume of the product is 200-300ml with platelet content of $>3X10^{11}$. Single unit is sufficient as an adult dose.

Who can donate platelets?

Almost all the criteria are the same as in the blood donation eligibility, except the time duration for platelet donation after any blood donation should be 28 days.

How often can you donate platelets?

As long as you are healthy and continue to meet the eligibility criteria, you can safely donate every 15 days. Many of our platelet donors schedule regular appointments every other week. While you can donate every 3 days, you can only donate platelets twice a month and not more than 24 times per year.

Is it safe to donate platelets?

At all times during the platelet collection process your blood remains inside a sterile tubing system and is never in contact with the equipment used for your platelet donation. All tubing, bags and the needle used to collect your platelets are new, sterile and used only once for you. After use, the entire disposable kit is discarded.

How long does it take to donate platelets?

Although your actual platelet donation will take approximately 45-75 minutes, please allow a total of at least two hours from registration through refreshments.

How to prepare for platelet donation

Just like donating blood, platelet donors need to get a good night's sleep on the night leading up to their donation. Unlike donating whole blood, you are required to avoid aspirin for 48 hours before donation, as it will affect the clotting properties of your platelets. Doctors also recommend that donors should drink fluids and have a full meal prior to your donation.

Stretching the stomach with a full meal opens the blood vessels around the stomach and constricts them in the rest of the body, resulting in an increased blood pressure. This helps you better tolerate a donation.

What happens when you donate platelets?

Platelets are donated through a process called platelet apheresis, which is much more efficient than gathering platelets from whole blood donations. (A single platelet treatment would require six to eight whole blood donors instead of just one platelet apheresis donor.) It is better for the patient because it reduces exposure to multiple donors.

The platelet donation process follows the same steps as whole blood donation registration, screening, donation and after-care.

What is apheresis?

Apheresis is the process by which platelets and other specific blood components (red cells or plasma) are collected from a donor. The word "apheresis" is derived from the Greek word aphaeresis meaning "to take away." This process is accomplished by using a machine called a cell separator. Blood is drawn from the donor and the platelets, or another blood component, are collected by the cell separator and the remaining components of the blood are returned to the donor during the donation. Each apheresis donation procedure takes about one-and-one-half to two hours. Donors can watch movies or relax during the donation.

Platelets life-span

It's 5 days. Means, donated platelet should be consumed within 5 days of the donation.

What should I do after donating blood?

(same as mentioned in Blood donation knowledge byte)

Myths and Facts about blood donations

(same as mentioned in Blood donation knowledge byte)

"Never refuse to donate Platelets if you can,
as you may be the next needy."

KNOWLEDGE BYTE 3

ORGAN DONATION

"After you die if you are buried you will be spoiled. If you are burnt you will become ash but if your body is donated you will live to offer life and bliss to several"

The Government of India enacted the Transplantation associated with the Human Organs Act within 1994 to change body organ trading & increase deceased body organ donation. Right after dealing with a multi billion rupee kidney scandal inside 2008, an amendment was suggested within 2009 as well as transferred this year to eliminate loopholes that in the past created unlawful body organ trading attainable.

Throughout 2019, the Government of India implemented the National Organ Transplant Programme having a low cost of Rs.149.5 crore (US$ twenty one million) for advertising deceased Organ donation.

Things for example not enough understanding (about mind death), faith, and also insufficient transplantation facilities impact the country's Organ donation plan.

The requirement for body organ donors has in no way been bigger. A lot more than 500,000 Indians are actually believed to remain for dreadful demand of a body organ transplant.

Based on the World Health Organization, just approximately 0.01 % of individuals within India donate the particular organs of theirs following demise.

The possibility of deceased body organ donations as a result of brain dead is loaded with the nation. Approximately 80,000 individuals expire because of street crashes each year. And believed 50% of these kinds of deaths are actually due to brain dead.

Are you aware?

In India every year nearly:

- 500,000 individuals expire due to non-availability of organs
- 200,000 individuals expire of liver disease
- 50,000 individuals expire with center disease
- 150,000 individuals await a kidney transplant but just 5,000 obtain one
- 1,000,000 citizens have corneal loss of sight and then await transplant Nevertheless, under a 1000 transplants coming from deceased donors are actually carried out every year - an insignificant and small incredible quantity as compared to the stats across the globe. Several of the individuals will locate an existing donor who'll donate a body organ for them. The majority will most likely run out watching for a body organ.

Here is what everyone should understand to alter the truth.

What exactly is body organ donation?

In order to know Organ Donation, it's crucial to understand Organ Transplants. A transplant is a surgical procedure in which a particular person's dysfunctional body organ or perhaps cells is in fact substituted by that of another individual. Transplants significantly enhance the caliber of living of this affected person..

While many organs which are transplanted come from deceased donors, people might also get organs via live donors. Even after death, kidney, parts of the liver, blood, intestines, pancreas, lung, still remain alive for some time.

One organ donor can donate up to twenty five different organs and tissues for transplantation. This can save up to nine lives!

How does body organ donation assist individuals with body organ disaster?

For body organ recipients, a transplant usually implies another possibility of living. Essential organs like, pancreas, liver, lungs and kidneys may be transplanted to the people whose organs are actually screwing up. For many, a body organ transplant does not need to be determined by pricey regular remedies to make it through. It allows for a lot of recipients to go back to a typical way of living. For example, a cornea transplant may enable a recipient to get back his vision.

What exactly are the various kinds of body organ donation?

A person can give consent to donate any particular organ of his body for transplant in his/her lifetime. When that person dies, the consented body part is taken and transplanted to the terminally ill person. A person may even wish to donate the entire body to a medical hospital or any suitable institution and thereby pave the way for extra lease of life for the ill person. However, the decision on whether a person can donate organ or not, rests on his or her medical examination. If that person is fully fit to donate, then and only then he (or she) can qualify for organ donation. Given below are the kinds of body organ donation:

1. **Living Donation:** Living donation happens each time an existing man or woman donates a body organ (or maybe a part of a body organ) for transplantation to someone else. The lifestyle donor is usually a member of the family, like a mom or dad, kid, daughter or brother, grandchild or grandparent (residing associated donation). It is able to additionally originate from somebody who's psychologically associated with the recipient, like a healthy buddy, a relative, an in law or a neighbor (living not related donation).
2. **Deceased Cadaver Donation:** The individual needs to register within a medical center which does transplants. The individual is going to be placed on a wait checklist. As and when the body organ comes from the ideal deceased donor (brain death) is purchased, the individual is intimated.

What organs could be donated?

Organs which could be donated include kidneys, liver, pancreas, heart and lungs, while cells comprises eyes, epidermis, bone, bone marrow, nervous feelings, mind, center regulators, eardrum, ear bones as well as blood.

What's India's place on body organ donations?

Body organ donations are actually authorized by Indian law. The Indian federal government enacted the Transplantation of Human Organs Act (THOA), 1994, that enabled body organ donation, as well as legalized the idea of' brain death'.

Vital Note: Brain demise isn't coma. Coma is actually an expression of rich unconsciousness, in which your brain will continue to perform and also the visitor is able to inhale on his/her to promote, minus the assistance of a ventilator. In the condition of coma, your brain continues to have the capability to fix.

Inside India, a board of four physicians has got to declare your brain dead ahead of the organs of yours could be harvested - this is accomplished following a number of exhaustive assessments- Cornea reflex check, Ear reflex test, Gag reflex check as well as Aphena reflex check - that are repeated two times inside a period of 6 hours. The board needs to consist of - the healthcare administrator, the leader of this medical center, an authorized professional, a neurologist/neurosurgeon and also the healthcare officer dealing with diligence. In many nations across the planet, the assessments are completed only one time.

The thing that makes body organ donation hard to find in India

Locating a donor is actually tough to start with. Inside India, this particular task is actually compounded by bureaucratic obstacles as well as not enough understanding.

The very first problem is lengthy and red-tapism. As stated by pre-existing guidelines, when the possibility donor isn't associated with the individual that requires the body organ, the transplant has to be accredited by the way of a state level committee or perhaps by the way of a medical center committee which has federal government officials.

The following problem is: it's usually hard for the medical professionals to persuade the household participants to donate the organs to a distant relative. Misconceptions, superstitions happen to be the major impediments, even when the loved ones get prepared to donate.

Another major issue is that majority of clinics of today are not conducive for transplants. Even surgeons are far from being adequately equipped and skilled to carry out a successful transplant.

Contrary to popular belief, organ donation doesn't disfigure the deceased donor's body. There's only one incision and organs are retrieved.

Good organs must be transplanted quickly using the donor to the recipient. Organs should be taken out quickly following the dedication of mind demise, while blood circulation should be taken care of synthetically. Tissue cells might be eliminated to twelve to twenty four several hours.

The donor's family group does not need to bear some costs for body organs or maybe cell donation. Every expense pertaining to the body organ transplant surgical treatment is going to be managed through the recipient's loved ones or maybe the organ transplant application.

Body organ donation anticipating prospect lists are designed based on the seriousness of these illness, blood sort, etc.

In contrast to several Western nations, in which a person is actually directed to create a decision in case he/she wishes to become a donor, inside India, the option is still left to the household. Following someone transporting a donor flash memory card expires, the household nonetheless has to approve the donation of organs. Thus, in case you plan to become a body organ donor, it's vital for you to inform the family of yours in connection with the wish of yours.

You will discover not many health conditions that will instantly disqualify you from donating some organs or even cells. And so, do not disqualify yourself!

How can you donate?

In order to be a body organ donor, it's essential to register for Organ Donation. One of them is required to fill up a recommended consent type, that may be either downloaded by using National Organ as well as Tissue Transplant Organization (NOTTO) site (https://www.notto.gov.in/) or even seen through the healthcare facility which is actually approached for body organ transplant. Just in case of deceased donation, a created consent type through the lawful custodian of this entire body following the demise of this individual is needed inside a recommended program type.

The possibility donor could also deal with body organ donation agencies for a donor flash memory card. While not legally binding, the donor flash memory card is actually a way of articulating sandals readiness to donate kidneys as well as generate loved ones much more comprehension towards the purpose. Until finally traveling licenses begin doubling in place as donor cards, 18x continues to be the most effective choice to make certain this one's organs are actually donated.

What's Green corridors?

Research has indicated that the risks of a transplantation achieving success are actually increased by decreasing enough lag time in between transplant as well as crop of this body organ.

Thus, commuter routes of this body organ are6 a crucial component. Because of this objective, "green corridors" were developed within numerous regions of India.

A "green corridor" describes a path which is actually cleared out there for an ambulance transporting the harvested organs to make sure that the shipping and delivery of it is on the spot within the least period attainable.

Use of eco-friendly corridors expedites body organ transplantations while simultaneously making certain there's absolutely no body organ food wastage.

However, the procedure of establishing an environmentally friendly corridor is actually complicated, because it calls for control of several stakeholders.

Because of the inconvenience to the general public when working with highways for that objective, more widespread use of atmosphere ambulances was recommended to the federal government.

"Carry on with eternal
life-promise to donate your body."

KNOWLEDGE BYTE 4

RIGHTS AND RESPONSIBILITIES OF PATIENTS

Overview of Patients' rights in India

1. Right to information.
2. Right to records and reports
3. Right to Emergency Medical Care
4. Right to informed consent
5. Right to confidentiality, human dignity and privacy.
6. Right to second opinion
7. Right to transparency in rates, and care according to prescribed rates wherever relevant
8. Right to nondiscrimination
9. Right to safety and quality care according to standards
10. Right to choose alternative treatment options if available
11. Right to choose source for obtaining medicines or tests

12. Right to proper referral and transfer, which is free from perverse commercial influences
13. Right to protection for patients involved in clinical trials
14. Right to protection of participants involved in biomedical and health research
15. Right to take discharge of patient, or receive body of deceased from hospital
16. Right to Patient Education
17. Right to be heard and seek redressal

(Source:http://clinicalestablishments.gov.in/WriteReadData/8431.pdf)

Responsibilities of patients and caretakers

Along with promoting their rights, patients and caretakers should follow their responsibilities so that hospitals and doctors can perform their work satisfactorily.

1. Patients should provide all required health related information to their doctor, in response to the doctor's queries without concealing any relevant information, so that diagnosis and treatment can be facilitated.
2. Patients should cooperate with the doctor during examination, diagnostic tests and treatment, and should follow doctor's advice, while keeping in view their right to participate in decision making related to treatment.
3. Patients should follow all instructions regarding appointment time, cooperate with hospital staff and fellow patients, avoid creating disturbance to other patients, and maintain cleanliness in the hospital.
4. Patients should respect the dignity of the doctor and other hospital staff as human beings and as professionals.

Whatever the grievance may be, patients/caregivers should not resort to violence in any form and damage or destroy any property of the hospital or the service provider.

5. The Patients should take responsibility for their actions based on choices made regarding treatment options, and in case they refuse treatment.

CONCLUSION

Let's join hands to make India "the country of the Millions of Real-life heroes" by 2025 where there will be zero incident when any operations/surgeries has been delayed due to non-availability of Blood/platelets.

ANNEXURE

Now registered free* for 1 year for Electronic Health Records service by visiting:

MDHL–My Digital Health Locker (https://app.mdhl.in/)

Or

Download the MDHL–My Digital Health Locker mobile application from play store or app store.

How does it work?

Step1: Register and Login with https://app.mdhl.in/get your unique MDHL I'd

Step 2: Print own Health Card [which will have your Name, Address, Age, emergency contact details, blood group, Mini Health History (allergies, blood pressure, diabetes....), Health

Insurance policy name and number, etc.], to carry your complete health records in your pocket/mobile.

Step 3: Upload all the records onto the secured digital Health Locker. In order to scan the documents, simply take a picture of them.

Or

Request your healthcare providers (or yourself) to Email all the health records to your unique MDHL I'd.

Step 4: Approve the Health records (to avoid spams).

Step 5: Whenever you need to access your medical records online, sign in or just enter your details to access them. You can view your personal health records online on the https://app.mdhl.in/

In case of emergency your healthcare providers can access the same if you allow (through OTP).

Five simple tips to safe storage of medicines at home and on-the-go:

1. **Choose a Safe Spot:** Walk around your house to find the safest place to keep your medicines. The location should be up and away and out of the sight and reach of young children.
2. **Lock the Safety Cap:** Always relock the cap on a medicine bottle. If the bottle has a locking cap that turns, twist it until you hear the click or cannot twist anymore.
3. **Put Medicines Away:** After locking the safety cap, it's important to always put medicines back in their safe storage location. Curious children act fast, so never leave medicine out on a kitchen counter or at a sick child's bedside, even if you have to give it again in a few hours.
4. Ask family members, houseguests, and other visitors to keep purses, bags, or coats that have medicine in them up and away and out of sight when they are in your home.
5. While staying with family or friends or at a hotel, find a safe storage place that is out of sight and reach of young children, like a high cabinet. If you're in a hotel room,

try the passcode-protected room safe for safe storage.

Now registered free* for 1 year for Electronic Health Records service by visiting:

MDHL–My Digital Health Locker (https://app.mdhl.in/)

Or

Download the MDHL–My Digital Health Locker mobile application from play store or app store.

How does it work?

Step1: Register and Login with https://app.mdhl.in/get your unique MDHL I'd

Step 2: Print own Health Card [which will have your Name, Address, Age, emergency contact details, blood group, Mini Health History (allergies, blood pressure, diabetes….), Health Insurance policy name and number, etc.], to carry your complete health records in your pocket/mobile.

Step 3: Upload all the records onto the secured digital Health Locker. In order to scan the documents, simply take a picture of them.

Or

Request your healthcare providers (or yourself) to Email all the health records to your unique MDHL I'd.

Step 4: Approve the Health records (to avoid spams).

Step 5: Whenever you need to access your medical records online, sign in or just enter your details to access them. You can view your personal health records online on the https://app.mdhl.in/

In case of emergency your healthcare providers can access the same if you allow (through OTP).

Hospital discharge Checklist

When leaving the hospital, make sure to get the following information:

1. **Settling the payment**
    a. Check and verify all the hospital services invoices
    b. Systematize all the prescriptions.
    c. Collect and verify all the pharmacy/medication invoices
    d. Collect all Laboratory/Diagnostic test results
    e. Collect and check discharge card
    f. Check all payment receipts.
2. **Hospital information**
    a. Floor no.
    b. Department name
    c. Bed no.
3. **Attending physician**
    a. Name
    b. Specialty
    c. Emergency contact number
4. **Hospital Pharmacy**
    a. Contact person
    b. Phone number
    c. Extension number
5. **Attending nurse**
    a. Name
    b. Phone number

    c. Extension number

6. **Follow-up appointments setup**
    a. Who will you be seeing?
    b. Date?
    c. Time?
7. **Follow-up care information - Who will you be talking to?**
8. **Discharge prescription**
    a. When was the last dose given?
    b. What changes were made to the prescription?
    c. Any notes or results

Road To Buy Best Health Insurance

(1) Determine your current needs

(2) Understand expenses you can afford can't afford

(3) Decide the members to be covered

(4) Fill detailed information to view comparison and quotes

(5) Research insurer and verify network hospitals and benefits

(6) Buy the selected policy

(7) Renew the policy on-time to avail benefits.

Making a health insurance claim

<table>
<tr><th>Steps</th><th>Planned</th><th>Emergency</th><th>Reimbursement policy</th></tr>
<tr><td>1.</td><td>Go to the hospital and present your insurance card</td><td>Get admitted to hospital. Present insurance card</td><td>Get admitted to hospital. Present insurance card</td></tr>
<tr><td>2.</td><td>Hospital coordinates with insurers</td><td>Hospital treats you</td><td>Hospital treats you.</td></tr>
<tr><td>3.</td><td colspan="2">Insurers ask documents from Hospital</td><td>You pay the hospital bills</td></tr>
<tr><td>4.</td><td colspan="2">Insurer authorize the procedure in line with your policy</td><td>Insurer ask for complete treatment records</td></tr>
<tr><td>5.</td><td colspan="2">You get treatment</td><td>Insurer ask for all invoices and receipt of the payment made</td></tr>
<tr><td>6.</td><td colspan="2">Insurers settle claim and bills</td><td>Insurers settle claim and reimburse according to Health policy</td></tr>
</table>

Prescriptions abbreviations https://hemangpajwani.com/rx-abbreviations.html

List of Insurance Company in India:

https://www.irdai.gov.in/ADMINCMS/cms/NormalData_Layout.aspx?page=PageNo129&mid=3.1.9

Blood bank list of India: https://cdsco.gov.in/opencms/resources/UploadCDSCOWeb/2018/UploadBloodBank/newBLOOD_BANKS_INDIA.pdf

Links to download forms for Organ Donation:

https://www.notto.gov.in/download-forms.htm

SOURCES

https://fit.thequint.com/

https://friends2support.org/

https://www.kokilabenhospital.com/

https://www.stmaryskc.com/

http://clinicalestablishments.gov.in/

https://www.thebetterindia.com/

https://www.indiatoday.in/

https://www.notto.gov.in/

https://en.wikipedia.org/

https://blogs.medibuddy.in/

https://www.quora.com/

https://www.cdc.gov/

https://blogs.webmd.com/

https://medlineplus.gov/

https://www.apollopharmacy.in/

https://www.pittsburghhealthcarereport.com/

https://www.drugs.com/

https://healthengine.com.au/

https://www.verywellhealth.com/

https://www.quora.com/

https://www.surgeryencyclopedia.com/

https://www.gethealthystayhealthy.com/

https://www.truenorthitg.com/

https://www.healthit.gov/

https://www.mayoclinic.org/

https://www.webmd.com/

https://capo.wildapricot.org/

http://www.bccancer.bc.ca/

https://www.moneycontrol.com/

https://mdhl/in